HAL·LEONARD INSTRUMENTAL PLAY-ALONG

ONLINE MEDIA INCLUDED
Audio Recordings
Printable Piano Accompaniments

PLAYBACK+
Speed • Pitch • Balance • Loop

CLASSICAL SOLOS FOR TROMBONE

15 Easy Solos for Contest and Performance

Arranged by Philip Sparke

T0081951

To access recordings and PDF accompaniments, visit:
www.halleonard.com/mylibrary

Enter Code
7652-8805-7229-8781

ISBN 978-1-61780-702-2

Visit Hal Leonard Online at
www.halleonard.com

Contact us:
Hal Leonard
7777 West Bluemound Road
Milwaukee, WI 53213
Email: info@halleonard.com

In Europe, contact:
Hal Leonard Europe Limited
42 Wigmore Street
Marylebone, London, W1U 2RN
Email: info@halleonardeurope.com

In Australia, contact:
Hal Leonard Australia Pty. Ltd.
4 Lentara Court
Cheltenham, Victoria, 3192 Australia
Email: info@halleonard.com.au

WALTZ

TROMBONE

MORITZ VOGEL
Arranged by PHILIP SPARKE

CHORALE
Now praise, my soul, the Lord

TROMBONE

JOHANN SEBASTIAN BACH
Arranged by PHILIP SPARKE

HUMMING SONG

from *Album for the Young*

TROMBONE

ROBERT SCHUMANN
Arranged by PHILIP SPARKE

GYMNOPÉDIE NO. 1

TROMBONE

ERIK SATIE
Arranged by PHILIP SPARKE

Andante (♩ = 96)

Small notes opt.

I'M CALLED LITTLE BUTTERCUP

from *HMS Pinafore*

SIR ARTHUR SULLIVAN
Arranged by PHILIP SPARKE

TROMBONE

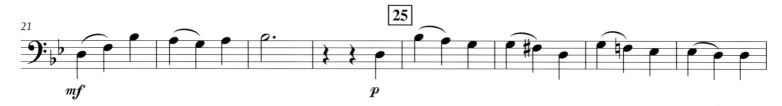

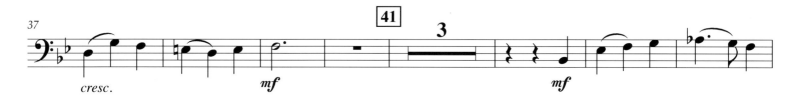

00842550

STUDY
Op. 37, No. 3

HENRY LEMOINE
Arranged by PHILIP SPARKE

TROMBONE

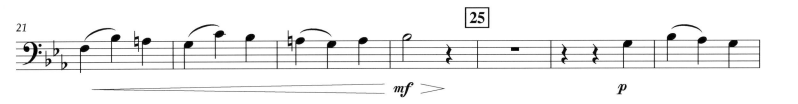

00842550

MINUET
(Z. 649)

HENRY PURCELL
Arranged by PHILIP SPARKE

TROMBONE

THEME AND VARIATION
from *Sonatina No. 3*

TROMBONE

THOMAS ATTWOOD
Arranged by PHILIP SPARKE

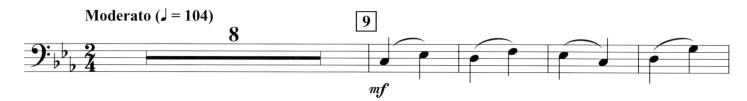

NORTHERN SONG

from *Album for the Young*

TROMBONE

ROBERT SCHUMANN
Arranged by PHILIP SPARKE

TWO GERMAN DANCES

from *Twelve German Dances, D. 420*

FRANZ SCHUBERT
Arranged by PHILIP SPARKE

TROMBONE

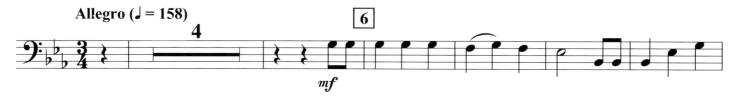

WATCHMAN'S SONG
from *Lyric Pieces, Op. 12*

EDVARD GRIEG
Arranged by PHILIP SPARKE

TROMBONE

Moderato (♩ = 104)

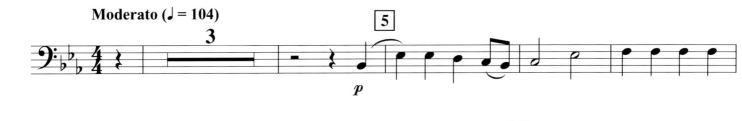

GAVOTTE

TROMBONE

JAN LADISLAV DUSSEK
Arranged by PHILIP SPARKE

VIEN QUÀ, DORINA BELLA

TROMBONE

ANTONIO BIANCHI
Transcribed by **C. M. von WEBER**
Arranged by PHILIP SPARKE

MINUET

from *Notebook for Anna Magdalena Bach*

Attributed to **CHRISTIAN PETZOLD**
Arranged by PHILIP SPARKE

TROMBONE

00842544

THE PRINCE OF DENMARK'S MARCH

from *Choice Lessons for the Harpsichord or Spinet*

JEREMIAH CLARKE
Arranged by PHILIP SPARKE

TROMBONE